MORE SUPER · SIMPLE SCIENCE ·

SCIENCE EXPERIMENTS WITH

MAGNETS

A Division of ABDO

ABDO
Publishing Company

BY ALEX KUSKOWSKI

Consulting Editor, Diane Craig, M.A./Reading Specialist

visit us at www.abdopublishing.com

Published by ABDO Publishing Company, a division of ABDO, P.O. Box 398166, Minneapolis, Minnesota 55439. Copyright © 2014 by Abdo Consulting Group, Inc. International copyrights reserved in all countries. No part of this book may be reproduced in any form without written permission from the publisher. Super SandCastle™ is a trademark and logo of ABDO Publishing Company.

Printed in the United States of America, North Mankato, Minnesota
062013
112013

 PRINTED ON RECYCLED PAPER

Editor: Liz Salzmann
Content Developer: Alex Kuskowski
Cover and Interior Design and Production: Mighty Media, Inc.
Photo Credits: Aaron DeYoe, Shutterstock

The following manufacturers/names appearing in this book are trademarks:
Fiskars®, Pyrex®, Rayovac®, Total®, Ziploc®

Library of Congress Cataloging-in-Publication Data
Kuskowski, Alex.
  Science Experiments with magnets / by Alex Kuskowski ; consulting editor, Diane Craig, M.A./ reading specialist.
    pages cm. -- (More super simple science)
  Audience: 5-10.
  ISBN 978-1-61783-853-8
1. Magnets--Juvenile literature. 2. Magnetism--Juvenile literature. I. Craig, Diane, editor. II. Title.
  QC757.5.K87 2014
  538--dc23
                    2012049960

Super SandCastle™ books are created by a team of professional educators, reading specialists, and content developers around five essential components—phonemic awareness, phonics, vocabulary, text comprehension, and fluency—to assist young readers as they develop reading skills and strategies and increase their general knowledge. All books are written, reviewed, and leveled for guided reading, early reading intervention, and Accelerated Reader® programs for use in shared, guided, and independent reading and writing activities to support a balanced approach to literacy instruction.

TO ADULT HELPERS

Learning about science is fun and simple to do. There are just a few things to remember to keep kids safe. Some activities in this book recommend adult supervision. Be sure to review the activities before starting, and be ready to assist your budding scientist when necessary.

KEY SYMBOLS

Look for these symbols in this book.

SHARP!
You will be working with a sharp object. Get help!

HOT!
You will be working with something hot. Get help!

TABLE OF CONTENTS

SUPER SIMPLE SCIENCE

You can be a scientist! It's super simple. Science is all around you. Learning about the world around you is part of the fun of science. Science is in your house, your backyard, and on the playground.

Find science in paper clips and clay. Look for science in bread and batteries. Try the activities in this book. You'll never know where to find science unless you look!

SCIENCE WITH MAGNETS

Use magnets to learn about science. Science explains how magnets work. Science shows you how to get metals out of food! In this book you will see how magnets can help you learn about science.

WORK LIKE A SCIENTIST

Scientists have a special way of working. It is a series of steps called the Scientific Method. Follow the steps to work like a scientist:

1. Look at something. What do you see? What does it do?

2. Think of a question about the thing you are watching. What is it like? Why is it like that? How did it get that way?

3. Think of a possible answer to the question.

4. Do a test to find out if you are right. Write down what happened.

5. Think about it. Were you right? Why or why not?

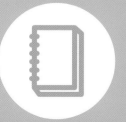

KEEP TRACK

There's another way to be just like a scientist. Scientists make notes about everything they do. So get a notebook. When you do an experiment, write down what happens in each step. It's super simple!

WHAT YOU WILL NEED

bowls

card stock & cardboard

chenille stems

clay

compass

copper wire

craft sticks

D battery

dinner knife

drinking glass & cups

drinking straw

fixative spray

gloves

glue & tape

ice

iron-fortified cereal

magnets (bar, donut, round, adhesive)

measuring cups

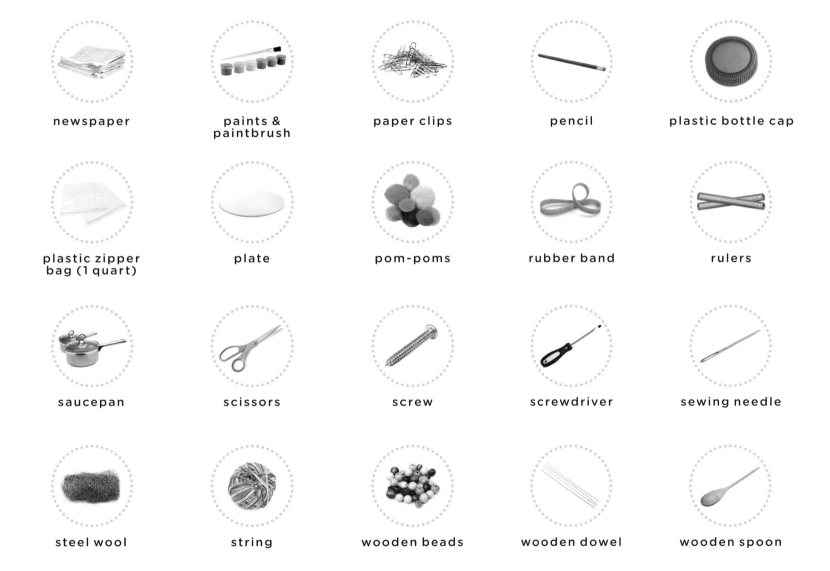

newspaper

paints & paintbrush

paper clips

pencil

plastic bottle cap

plastic zipper bag (1 quart)

plate

pom-poms

rubber band

rulers

saucepan

scissors

screw

screwdriver

sewing needle

steel wool

string

wooden beads

wooden dowel

wooden spoon

MAGIC FLOATING MAGNETS

WHAT YOU WILL NEED

clay

wooden dowel

6 donut magnets

DIRECTIONS

① Roll the clay into a ball. Make it about as wide as the magnets. Flatten the ball slightly. Stick the dowel into the clay.

② Stack the magnets. Pick up the top two magnets. Do not turn them over. Put them on the dowel.

③ Pick up the next two magnets. Turn them upside down. Put them on the dowel.

4 Put the last two magnets on the dowel. Do not turn them over.

WHAT'S GOING ON?

A magnet has a north pole and a south pole. Opposite poles **attract** each other. Matching poles push away from each other. This makes the magnets float.

A MAGNETIC CONNECTION

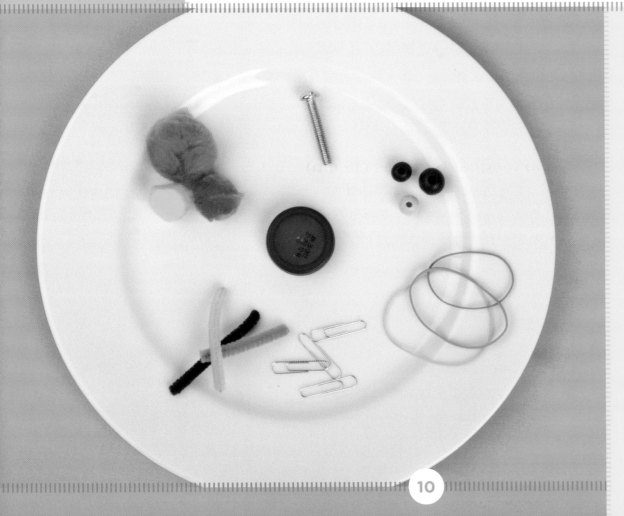

WHAT YOU WILL NEED

plate

screw

rubber band

paper clips

plastic bottle cap

chenille stems

wooden beads

pom-poms

bar magnet

ruler

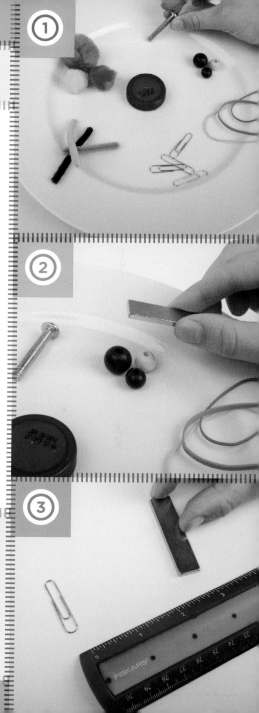

DIRECTIONS PART 1

1. Put all the **items** except the magnet and ruler on the plate. Are any of them drawn together?

2. Hold the magnet very close to each of the items. Don't let it touch them. What happens?

3. Put the paper clip and magnet 6 inches (15 cm) apart. Slowly move the magnet toward the paper clip. How far apart are they when the paper clip begins to move?

WHAT'S GOING ON?

Magnets are **attracted** to metals such as iron and steel. They can pick up objects made from those metals. Strong magnets can even move metal objects that are far away.

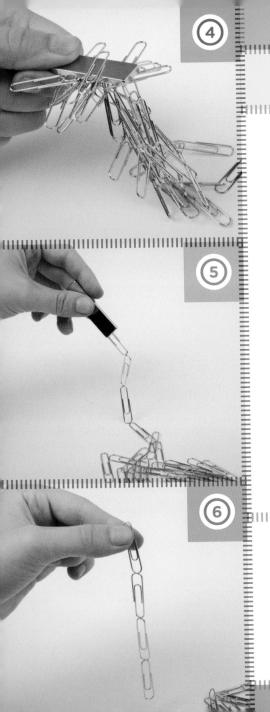

DIRECTIONS PART 2

④ Hold the magnet over a pile of paper clips. Count how many paper clips it picked up.

⑤ Now put one paper clip on the magnet. Use it to pick up other paper clips. **Attach** as many paper clips as possible.

⑥ Take the first paper clip off the magnet. What happens?

WHAT'S GOING ON?

Magnets can magnetize some metals. The first paper clip became a small magnet. It picked up other metals. It held them up even after the magnet was removed.

03 HOT 'N' COLD MAGNET PULL

WHAT YOU WILL NEED

2 bar magnets

paper clips

saucepan

measuring cup

water

wooden spoon

bowl

ice

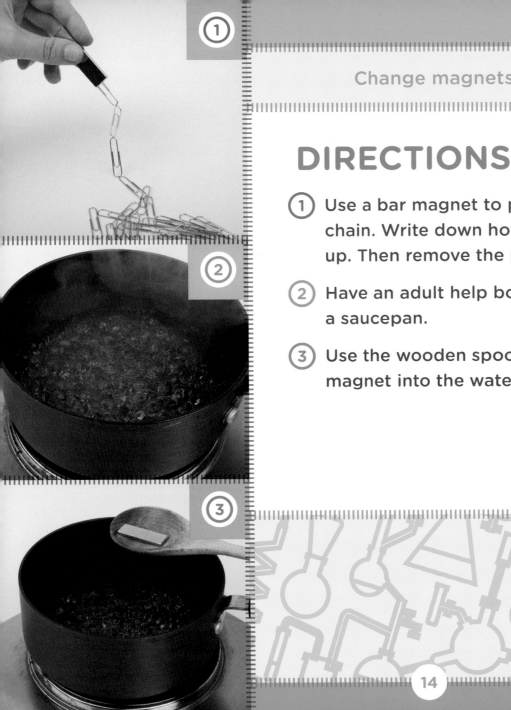

DIRECTIONS PART 1

1. Use a bar magnet to pick up paper clips in a chain. Write down how many paper clips it picks up. Then remove the paper clips.

2. Have an adult help boil 2 cups of water in a saucepan.

3. Use the wooden spoon to carefully lower the magnet into the water. Let it boil for 20 minutes.

DIRECTIONS PART 2

④ Fill the bowl with ice. Put the other bar magnet in it. Let it sit for 20 minutes.

5 Use the wooden spoon to remove the magnet from the hot water. Let the magnet cool completely.

⑥ Use the hot magnet to pick up paper clips like you did in step 1. Count how many it picks up.

⑦ Take the magnet out of the ice. Use it to pick up paper clips. Which magnet picked up the most? Which picked up the least?

WHAT'S GOING ON?

A magnet's strength is affected by temperature. Very hot and very cold magnets pick up fewer things. Some magnets can even stop working!

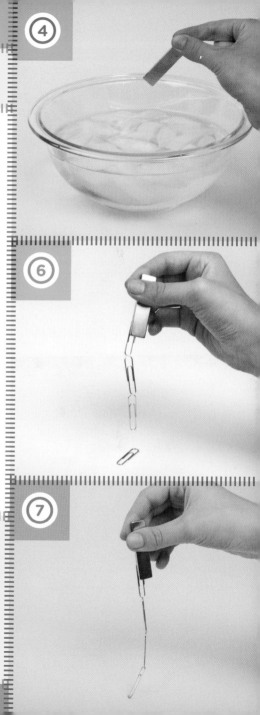

04 LOSING ALL DIRECTION

WHAT YOU WILL NEED

2 rulers

compass

tape

bar magnet

donut magnet

small round magnet

DIRECTIONS

1. Place a ruler on either side of the compass. Tape the rulers to the table.

2. Put the bar magnet at one end of a ruler. Move it closer until the compass needle starts to spin. Which way does the needle point?

3. Repeat step 2 with the other two magnets.

4. Put the donut magnet and bar magnet at the ends of the rulers. Slowly move them closer to the middle. When does the compass needle begin to move? Repeat with the donut magnet and the small round magnet.

WHAT'S GOING ON?

A compass is magnetic. It points to the closest, strongest magnet. Usually the needle points to the north pole. But a closer magnet can make the needle point in a different direction.

PLENTY OF FISH IN THE SEA

WHAT YOU WILL NEED

cardboard

paints

paintbrush

pencil

card stock

scissors

adhesive magnet

bar magnet

DIRECTIONS

1   Paint the cardboard blue. Decorate it like an ocean scene. Let the paint dry.

②   Draw a fish on card stock. Decorate it. Let the paint dry. Cut the fish out.

③   Peel the paper off the adhesive magnet. Stick it to the back of the fish. Press it on firmly.

④   Put the fish on the cardboard facing up. Hold the bar magnet against the back of the cardboard. Move the magnet back and forth. What happens?

WHAT'S GOING ON?

Magnets can **attract** each other through other objects, such as cardboard. When one magnet moves, the other magnet moves with it. It makes the fish swim!

MAGNETISM TAKES A BREAK

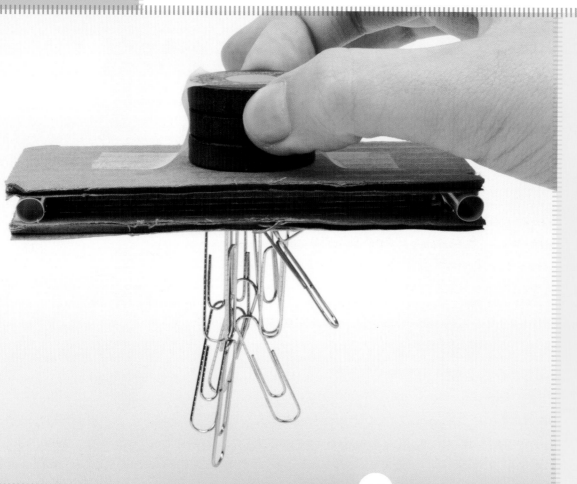

WHAT YOU WILL NEED

cardboard

ruler

scissors

drinking straw

glue

3 donut magnets

tape

paper clips

craft stick

dinner knife

Turn a magnet on and off!

DIRECTIONS

1   Cut two pieces of cardboard. Make them 4 inches (10 cm) by 2 inches (5 cm). Cut two pieces of straw 2 inches (5 cm) long.

2   Put glue along the short edges of one cardboard piece. Put the straws on the glue. Glue the other cardboard piece on top of the straws.

3   Let the glue dry. Tape three donut magnets on top of the cardboard.

4   Hold the cardboard by the magnets. Place it on top of some paper clips. Lift up the cardboard. Move a craft stick between the cardboard pieces. Repeat with the dinner knife.

WHAT'S GOING ON?

The paper clips are **attracted** to the magnet through the cardboard. The wooden craft stick doesn't affect it. But the metal knife blocks the magnetism. It makes the paper clips fall.

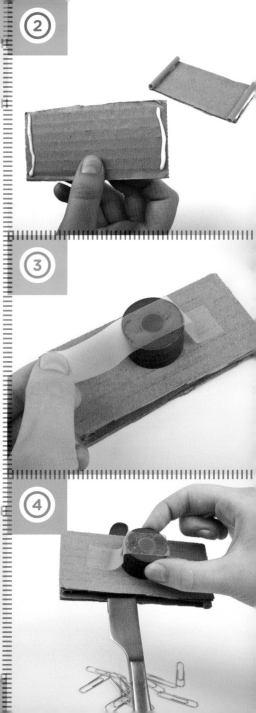

PORTRAIT OF A MAGNET

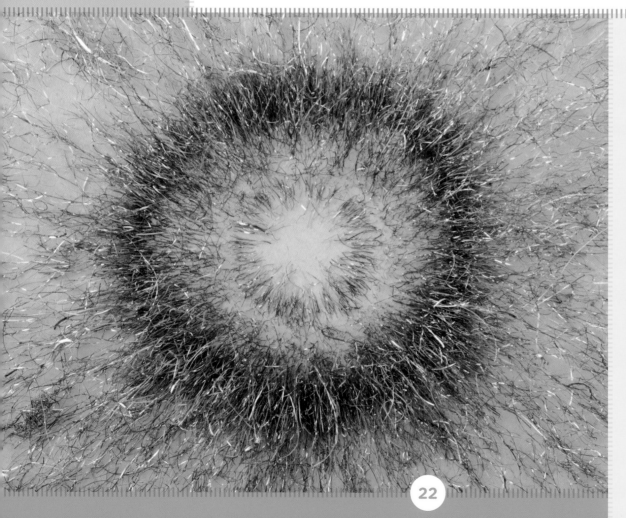

WHAT YOU WILL NEED

magnet

tape

card stock

newspaper

2-inch square steel wool

scissors

gloves

clear fixative spray

DIRECTIONS

1. Tape the magnet to one side of the card stock. Turn the card stock over. Put it on newspaper.

2. Have an adult cut the steel wool. Cut it into tiny pieces. Let the pieces fall on the card stock.

3. Wear gloves. Tap the card stock gently a couple of times. The steel wool will move toward the magnet.

4. Have an adult spray the card stock with clear fixative. Wait 2 hours. Spray it again. Let it dry. Take the magnet off.

WHAT'S GOING ON?

Magnets have magnetic fields. That's how far away a magnet **reacts** with metals. Steel wool is made from metal. The steel wool shows the magnetic field of the magnet.

THE STRANGE ATTRACTOR

WHAT YOU WILL NEED

string

ruler

scissors

donut magnets

pencil

2 cups, 4 inches (10 cm) tall

tape

DIRECTIONS

① Cut a string 3 inches (7.5 cm) long. Tie one end to a donut magnet. Tie the other end to the center of a pencil.

② Place the cups upside down. Tape one end of the pencil to each cup.

③ Make three stacks of donut magnets. Place them in a triangle between the cups. Space them 1 inch (2.5 cm) apart.

4 Gently push the hanging magnet. Watch it swing.

WHAT'S GOING ON?

Gravity and magnets act together. The hanging magnet is a **pendulum**. It swings in a pattern over the magnets. It is **attracted** to all of the magnets equally.

COOL WATER COMPASS

WHAT YOU WILL NEED

- bowl
- water
- sewing needle
- bar magnet
- plastic cap
- compass

DIRECTIONS

1   Fill the bowl with water.

2   Hold the needle by the eye. Rub the magnet along the needle from the eye to the tip. Keep rubbing for 2 minutes. Go in the same direction each time.

3   Put the plastic cap on the water with the top down.

4   Balance the needle on top of the cap. Watch the needle for 1 minute. What happens to the sharp end? Compare the sharp end to the compass.

WHAT'S GOING ON?

Earth's north pole is a magnet. Magnets **attract** each other. Rubbing the needle with the magnet magnetized it. It made the sharp end point to the north pole.

 HEAVY METAL BREAKFAST

WHAT YOU WILL NEED

iron-fortified cereal

measuring cup

1-quart plastic zipper bag

drinking glass

water

bar magnet

DIRECTIONS

1. Put 2 cups **cereal** in the plastic bag. Close the bag. Roll the glass over the bag to crush the cereal. Break the cereal into tiny pieces.

2. Add 2 cups of water. Close the bag. Shake to mix.

3. Hold the magnet in your palm. Place the bag on top. Move the liquid gently back and forth for 10 seconds.

4. Turn the bag over so the magnet is on top. Slowly pick up the magnet.

WHAT'S GOING ON?

The small black specks inside the bag are iron. They were in the cereal. The magnet pulled the iron out of the cereal mixture!

A MAGNET OF YOUR OWN

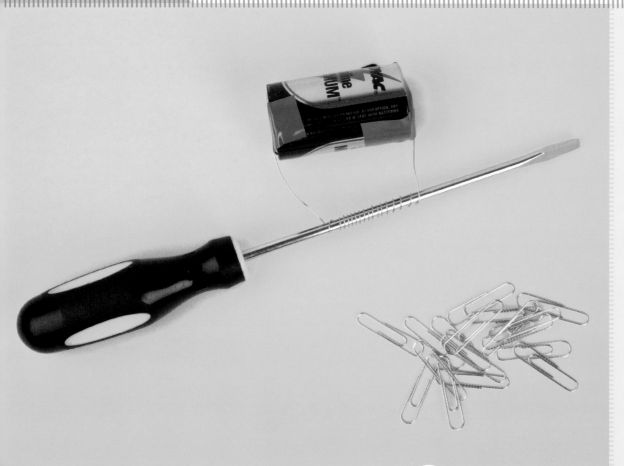

WHAT YOU WILL NEED

screwdriver

paper clips

15 inches (38 cm) copper wire

ruler

D battery

tape

DIRECTIONS

1   Touch the screwdriver to a paper clip. What happens?

2   Wrap the copper wire tightly around the metal part of the screwdriver. Leave 2 inches (5 cm) of each end of the wire unwrapped.

3   Tape each end of the wire to one end of the battery.

4   Hold the battery in one hand. Hold the screwdriver in the other hand. Touch the screwdriver to a paper clip again. What happens?

WHAT'S GOING ON?

An **electrified** wire wrapped around metal creates a magnetic field. The battery and wire turn the screwdriver into a magnet.

CONCLUSION

You just found out that science can be super simple! And you did it using magnets. Keep your thinking cap on! What other experiments can you do with magnets?

GLOSSARY

attach – to join or connect.

attract – to cause someone or something to come near.

cereal – a breakfast food usually made from grain and eaten with milk.

electrified – charged or filled with electricity.

item – a thing or object.

pendulum – something hanging from a single point so it can swing freely back and forth.

react – to move or behave in a certain way because of something else.